>:))

Emoticon Poetry

Cam Kalra

*Dedicated to those friends who inspired me, our lives were meant to intertwine…;-**

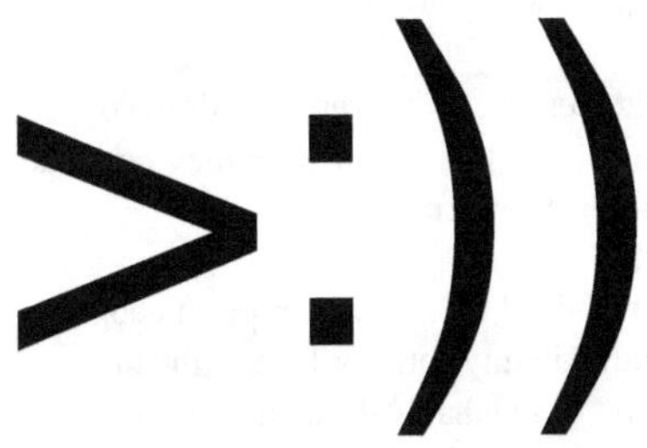

Emoticon Poetry

Cam Kalra

Halbaffe Press

First published 2020 by
HALBAFFE PRESS

Halbaffe Press in the US is an imprint of Sinensis Publications, a division of Sinensis LLC, registered in the USA. 5905 Washburn Avenue, Minneapolis, Minnesota 55406

ISBN-13: 978-0-578-71572-8

10 9 8 7 6 5 4 3 2

Contents

Forward

I started with a couple poems that just had to have emoticons as titles, there was no other way to express the intangible yet flippant rawness of emotions. Especially since as they started out hand-written, scrawled in a notepad around midnight, circa 2012, as I described emotions between pagan friends and I, that I couldn't really put words to.

I showed the poems to a writer's workshop years later and got encouragement to write out more in the same style, all with emoticon titles…

After editing this set of poems, I realized that I had to give a disclaimer, there's more fiction here than before. Sometimes as writers, our imaginations guide us like children. Half of what I write

about is the sublime or intangible,
and it's hard to write about when
my logical side wants to also write,
don't touch this, don't go there.
When dealing with life, death, and
the sacred, a lot of it can be
intangible and indescribable.

A lot of people inspired me,
along with my imagination. I hope
to create more memories with the
friends referred to here.
I also hope my poetry
encourages readers to create
magic in their own lives or at least
inspires creativity.

Much love,
Cam Kalra

Section 1

:-P

no cover charge
just pay for drinks
and lap dances
dingy low lighting

young women with
prominent
futures
and low life
mingle

an imam on his phone
by the bar
lying
about where he is

trying to convince
"Bunny"
to pursue
a degree in
web development

A crazy-looking dude
gets a lap dance
as we comment from afar

As we leave,
the imam is still
on the phone

:)

you realize
i'm tired of you
but so the honeymoon
might be over,
but it's not bad,
in context

i try to hide it from you,
to spare your feelings,
but you knew

but otherwise,
nothing is wrong

<...3

Sis,
between
the shrimp pad thai
and an unwavering
tenacity to survive,
we have
a mutually
symbiotic
kinesis
we can't
describe.

unspoken love

*:

Raised on separate
continents,
two lives lived apart
together

when you were little,
i made up my mind
that i would
patiently wait
for you to mature
until we could
have a conversation
without horseplay

#)

NYE.
You're doing readings
at some exclusive
party nearby

i'm at our usual club
met 2 nice guys
but they both had gfs
and didn't tell us
until the night was
practically over

:-/

Humid scantily clad nights
we argue about food
reminisce about
past birthdays
you want more info
'bout K.
Twerking in the
living room
till 2,
a brief oasis
in the dark

suddenly it's bright
you're late for work
I'm chatting up
new friends at the bus stop
you abruptly get up and leave
as I fumble with slips of
paper and
strangers

</3

it's 3am
I answer my phone
in a panic
but it's just you
wanting to chat.
who's the guy
you're crying about
who left you
for the 'crack whores'
tonight?
Just cuss him out
and move on
Tomorrow is a new day.

\>:(

I love you
more than is
healthy
to love
a clingy woman
who gets "visions"
and borrows money
she can't pay back.
Crazy sexy bitch,
pick who you want to be,
and write it on the back
of your hand
for easy reference.

X((

Sometimes I wake up
from a bad dream
where,
in your confusion,
you've forgotten
who I am
and white magic
is not your choice
weapon.

;-*

Laying there
In the dark,
cackling about
that sinister halo
from the radio,

no sane person
no offense
can sleep here
but didn't think
you'd try to get me
high either

=p

cozy winter nights

we came over
at night
booze and chicken

you told S my secret!
I trusted you
I wasn't trying
to flirt with you,
weird

hijinks till 3?
with that dang parrot
there the whole time

then a group of us
headed over
to Perkins for card games
till 6am

:((

we meet up again
like old times,
you still want to walk
to the club,

I get winded,
though i'm younger,
my back starts to pinch.
we get there,
i want to sit outside
try to recoup,
call a ride home

sky turns shades
of pink and orange,
why are we at the club
during the day?

;-$

intangible
aching
yearning,
to be
within,
to embrace
such toothsome
bittersweet
melancholy
in our very arms,

nuzzle my neck,
brücke, return
the warmth

as i pass out
on my desk,
this is fitting.

(:

i love that
you think
your blood type
(O positive)
makes you immune to
corona

if only
because hope
gives us reason
to go on.

hope you don't ever get sick

,"
,

are you fucking serious
right now?

how can you
avoid saying
i love you
to a kid
though
you do
love them?

talk! speak!
get it out!
like puking,
it'll make you
feel better

¯_(ツ)_/¯

calling me at work,
to rant at me
about how i organized
my own birthday

then calling me back
a week later,
also at work,
to apologize
and inform me
i made a good decision

okay, thanks

:D))

Fred never heard of you.
you told me
to drop your name,
and tell him that
you sent me,
but i already got
a deal done
before you called.
also he doesn't know you.

};-)

chatting with you
over text
feeling like,
there's something
in the air,
you felt it too
then i spoke from
the heart,
and without a clue,
it fell apart
around me

you apologized
later to no
avail

: ###

i left your place
that morning,
and slipped on ice

that same
evening
we met up
again,
and ate
in the snow.

i think you have
a stomach
of steel,
or i ate expired
mayo?

i had food poisoning
for 3 weeks

with my gut emptied
of everything
but e.coli
i was empty
of you,
for you

:l

you convinced me
to follow your friend
but that guy
wasn't anyone
you knew,
and my trust
and naïveté
got lost in translation

moments later,
i stepped
on a nail or
something
on my way back,

as sparrows
chattered above
enveloped in anticipation
of dawn

:-,

i think u offered me acid
but i didn't understand

my sweet tooth was not happy

we walked down the street
as you told your story
that made less sense
bit by bit

faces merged
stories collided

i laid down to sleep
on a piece of astroturf

i was a little wary after that

=D

chickadee email
is not a thing

i told myself
as i waited on
a short wall,

a church
retaining wall

a man walked
as poops
fell out his pant leg

upwards
the universe was a spiral
leaving a neat imprint
like people driving
early morning
commute

the spider legs
but it was lavender
so all cool

in hindsight,
maybe i have no clue where
that was

:+

massive art project.
cutting
and writing
valentines
for two hundred
strangers

good times,
though badly
planned

i love you
like Ricky Martin
loves trees

:')

seeing his baby
was very nice
but i felt overwhelmed
("overvhelmed")

her laziness
was palpable

but that wasn't the end

:X

we had to sit
and let ourselves go

build ourselves up
from the ground up

not just sit on our loins
and take it all for granted

we had to find who we were
to balance who we must be

that's it from the ground up.

Section 2

X-P

when it
drives me
when it
pushes me
when it
flows through me

then i know that i'm alive

:)(

got off a train
saw you standing there,

confusion still lingered,
though you are the one
that i wanted
all along

so happy,
finally together
though you
are too shy
for your own good

I wanted this
but didn't know
we were
already together,

screaming internally

:\\

the mailman
was nice
a total gent

tho he offered me
10 for 6
out of nowhere

i kinda had higher hopes
for that interaction
but hey, ya know?

:'l

Laying on your bed
in the afternoon
reading a book
such serenity,
didn't force
the drama
to come

:-}

At your place,
you made me dinner
orgasmic potatoes
and greens,
over a year
after we broke up,
we would still debate
how you made those
potatoes.

I think at one point
you were cheating,
but you're a great cook
Alas

:=/

We made plans to go
to the lake,
I didn't realize
fam would tag along.

you told me
in broken english
stories,
lost in translation,
about aliens, fruit,
and snakes.

Did you
grow up in a
cult??
Did I misunderstand?

Dating without borders.

:'"o

You told me
you didn't work
because a work injury

so grandma paid your rent
but when someone
broke into
your apartment
you blamed me??

years later
i met your roommate
a dealer, and his client.

I passed by you
in the hallway,
no time to ask
about grandma.

;-}

dragged you two
to the library
to give a tour,
but he doesn't
get it,

you and i chat
all the time,
anyway,
this is just
another place
to sit.

<__3

planning weddings
before and after
funerals,
at the bus stop,
all winter long,

every stereoscopic
detail,
life-giving nuance,
what if—
color schemes,
shower gifts, guest-list,
butterfly release,
nature setting
had to work

:3

girl,
you give
me life.
two little
elf-bums,
getting rides
bumping cigs,
chatting up djs,
hoping to get
into the guest list
or an after party.
we didn't do much
else.

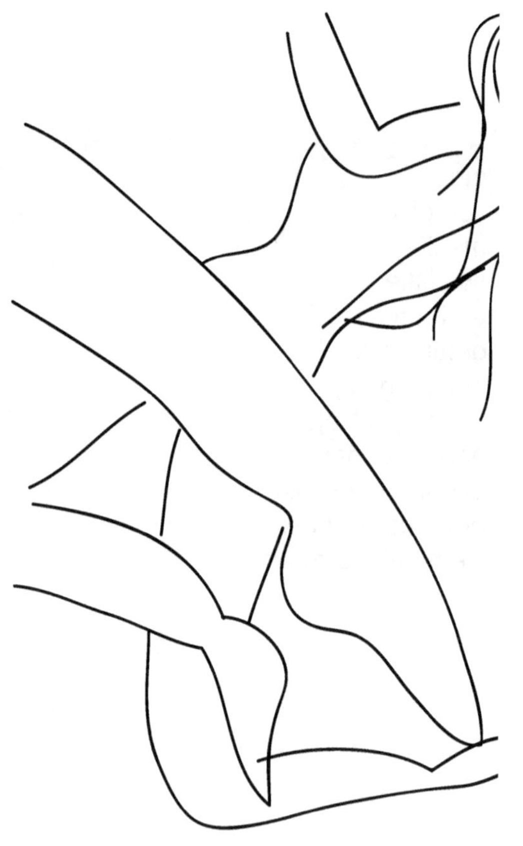

:-&

Love you, tho
U dragged me to your event
a group thing
i never knew about
not my scene
#respect

never talk about it,
never tell,
still tryin' to
delete this pics
off my iCloud

not my scene
but I love you

@ :/

the time i bought
a tattoo gun and kit
off amazon,
#obsessed with tats

tested it on some fruit,
you kept the orange

S wanted to be
my guinea pig
came back to earth
and needed safety

cooled off a little after that

:D

went to a rave
for my birthday
with an alcoholic

didn't see him the rest
of the night

didn't post about it
anywhere,
kept my phone mum

it was good,
such a long night
but chill

when you're young
and you need a beat
to breathe
clubbing can be
dangerous

my drunk companion
drove me home
as the sun rose

D":

Saturday night
at the club

My fave xdresser is there,
this one bud and
his roommates are there,
friends of friends already
on the dance floor.
So-and-so's
mom shows up.

I run into classmates,
and some guy who was
there last night too.

Around midnight
we form a conga line
around the room
chanting gibberish

Welcome to Mayberry.

0:))

Giving out
bad haircuts
thanksgiving
afternoon

so i kinda shaved
part of the idiot's head
but he was vague
and using terms
no one has heard

so he fully
shaved his head
and wore a hat in shame
to his gf's house
refusing to tell
anyone
what happened.

not my deal

someone that insecure
needed to grow up
sooner.

:$

finally
got ur driver's license
only to get into
an accident
not your fault
the other guy
had a stolen car
zero insurance

and being so petite,
you had to shove
yourself
so far against
the wheel
to reach the pedals,
that your boobs
got bruised
from the impact,
yet told no one

I-O

we met at a
dive bar
near campus,
to eat and map out
future projects.

i was too shy to say that
i missed you
hardcore

u were bring difficult
and nothing i said made
a difference anyway

we went to the warehouse
and worked on projects,
you gave me a couple
little funny trinkets

it would have been
easier to say
i love u

>:[

After we decided
to start dating,
you couldn't
stop mentioning
your ex,
literally
every few minutes.

Kinda hilarious
at first,
then I realized
you needed to talk.

8-0

i couldn't believe
we were sitting
on a park bench
you greeted
all the homeless
as you rolled
piles of cigs

it was a beautiful day
as we argued
abt a text msg,

after that,
i vowed to
never text you
in english again,
had to translate
every argument
every joke.

google translate
was a wall
between us

:")

Sitting in a coffee shop
reading and
drinking two lattes after
two months
of no caffeine

I waited for you,
you didn't show,
broken english
had happened.

Meanwhile,
in my book,
I read the word,
"yoga"
and a portal
opened over
my right shoulder,
to the 4th, 5th
and 6th dimensions
all at once.

Took me a while
to realize
what was going on

I was also
mad at you
for flaking.

8D

So, as I sat
and waited for you
I also realized
there was a feeling
like i was finally

something about
the music
the chill vibe
the raver clothes
being sold in a corner
made me feel like
i had arrived

I think I had
to be alone
to finally feel it

:-

in the 90's
there was a time
when ambient music
got popular,
and i was
secretly jealous
of people who got to
go to raves in sf

and that was here and
now

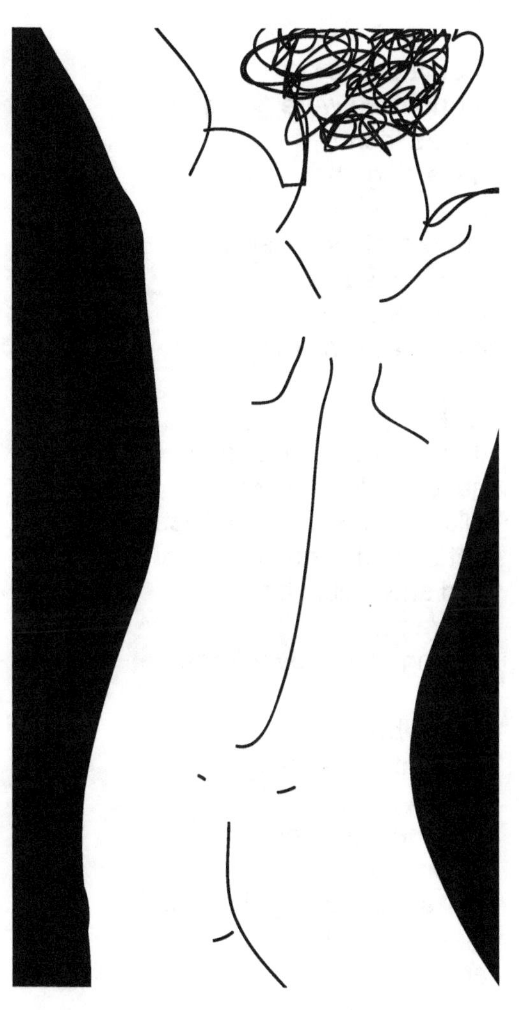

=\

took a bus to chi
thought we were going
to see friends,
have a lighthearted
quick trip
but two of us got sick
from not eating
in the end
had a fever of 104

took a bus to chi
thought we could see the city
have a little vacation
take a break from our lives,
got coated in grime
and saw a little bit
of drama
among other adventures

took a bus to chi
thought i was going
to see you again.
four months later
30 pounds lighter,
you started telling the truth.
I learned more
about myself
than anyone else
our love is strong
but you push it to the limit.

:""}

walking at 4am
looking for a friend,
meeting a guy,
discussing
his pal, G
over writing
as he bums
used cig butts

the city awakens
around us,
like in a bowl.

0:}

long nights
scurried away
figuring the
religious
ramifications
of transgender
rights, or,
right to exist?

hope against hope
that a God
of our childhood
loves us back

is it a
sin to
love oneself?
or a bigger
sacrilege
to not?

This book was printed in Helvetica 11 pt. It's a sans-serif font used on the web and in print, used here to give the feeling of reading on device screens.

www.ingramcontent.com/pod-product-compliance
Lightning Source LLC
Chambersburg PA
CBHW051007050726

47592CB00007B/2748